50 DECADENT QUICHE RECIPES

By
Brenda Van Niekerk

Copyright © 2012 Brenda Van Niekerk
All rights reserved.

ISBN-13:978-1500476250
ISBN-10:1500476250

Content

Spinach And Pistachio Quiche 7
Swiss Chard And Cheddar Quiche 9
Spinach, Walnut And Stilton Quiche 10
Blue Cheese And Pecan Nut Quiche 12
Pepper Quiche 13
Sausage And Cheese Quiche 14
Pizza Quiche 16
Broccoli And Ham Quiche 17
Feta And Spinach Quiche 18
Bacon And Leek Quiche 19
Rosemary, Chicken And Mushroom Quiche 21
Asparagus Quiche 23
Tuna And Corn Quiche 25
3 Cheese And Onion Quiche 27
Spicy Chorizo Sausage Quiche..28
Cranberry, Walnut And Brie Quiche 30
Chicken And Leek Quiche..31
Bacon And Zucchini Quiche..32
Gruyere, Bacon And Maple Quiche......................................34
Lamb And Mint Quiche 36
Blue Cheese And Fresh Herb Quiche 38
Mushroom Gruyere Quiche 39
Seafood Quiche...41
Sweet Chili Crab Quiche..43
Caramelized Onion, Feta And Walnut Quiche 45
Mini Bacon And Cheese Quiches 47
Lobster Quiche..48
Apple, Walnut And Blue Cheese Quiche 50
Gruyere, Pear And Ham Quiche 51
Artichoke Quiche 53
Zucchini And Red Pepper Quiche..55

Blueberry, Feta And Almond Quiche 57
Bacon And Oyster Quiche 58
Eggplant, Ham And Mozzarella Quiche 60
Potato Quiche 62
Salmon, Dill And Feta Quiche 64
Tomato And Fresh Basil Quiche 66
Butternut, Feta And Bacon Quiche 68
Chicken, Walnut And Pear Quiche 69
Salmon And Pea Quiche 71
Quiche Lorraine 73
Haddock And Corn Quiche 75
Gorgonzola And Caramelized Onion Quiche 77
Pancetta And Asparagus Quiche 79
Turkey And Broccoli Quiche 81
Sage, Apple And Sausage Quiche 83
Artichoke, Lemon Thyme And Parmesan Quiche 85
Gorgonzola And Roasted Fig Quiche 86
Feta, Strawberry And Black Pepper Quiche 88
Chicken And Cashew Quiche 90

SPINACH AND PISTACHIO QUICHE

INGREDIENTS

95,5 ml shortening
250 ml flour
2 ml salt
37,5 ml cold water
250 ml spinach (chopped and cooked for 1 minute)
125 ml Parmesan cheese (grated)
250 ml Gruyere cheese (grated)
125 ml pistachio nuts (chopped)
4 eggs (beaten)
500 ml whipping cream
3 ml salt
3 ml ground black pepper
50 ml fresh dill (chopped)

METHOD

Cut the shortening into the flour and salt.

Add the water 12,5 ml at a time.

Keep adding the water until the pastry almost cleans the side of the bowl (add more water if necessary).

Gather the pastry into a ball and place on a floured board.

Roll the pastry into circles larger than the quiche dish.

Place the pastry into the greased quiche dish.

Trim the overhanging edges of the pastry.

Pinch off the edges to neaten the pastry.

Arrange the spinach in the pastry-lined quiche dish.

Sprinkle the Parmesan cheese, Gruyere cheese, dill and pistachios over the spinach.

Beat the eggs, cream, black pepper and salt together.

Pour the egg mixture into the quiche dish.

Bake at 425 degrees F for 15 minutes.

Reduce the oven temperature to 300 degrees F.

Bake for a further 30 minutes.

SWISS CHARD AND CHEDDAR QUICHE

INGREDIENTS

8 eggs
125 ml sour cream
125 ml milk
250 ml Swiss chard (chopped and cooked for 1 minute)
250 ml strong cheddar cheese (grated)
5 ml salt
5 ml ground black pepper
4 spring onions (cleaned and chopped)
5 ml garlic (minced)

METHOD

Beat the eggs well.

Combine the sour cream and milk together.

Combine the eggs, salt, black pepper and the sour cream mixture together.

Add the cheddar cheese, garlic, spring onions and Swiss chard.

Mix well.

Pour the mixture into a greased oven dish.

Bake at 350° F for 25 to 30 minutes.

SPINACH, WALNUT AND STILTON QUICHE

INGREDIENTS

95,5 ml shortening
250 ml flour
2 ml salt
37,5 ml cold water
250 ml spinach (cooked, chopped and thoroughly drained)
250 ml Stilton (crumbled)
125 ml Parmesan cheese (grated)
125 ml walnuts (chopped)
83 ml onion (peeled and finely chopped)
10 ml fresh thyme (chopped)
4 eggs (beaten)
500 ml whipping cream
3 ml salt
2 ml ground black pepper
2 ml paprika

METHOD

Cut the shortening into the flour and salt.

Add the water 12,5 ml at a time.

Keep adding the water until the pastry almost cleans the side of the bowl (add more water if necessary).

Gather the pastry into a ball and place on a floured board.

Roll the pastry into circles larger than the quiche dish.

Place the pastry into the greased quiche dish.

Trim the overhanging edges of the pastry.

Pinch off the edges to neaten the pastry.

Sprinkle the spinach, walnuts, Parmesan cheese, Stilton, thyme and onion into the pastry-lined quiche dish.

Beat the eggs, cream, salt, paprika and black pepper together.

Pour the egg mixture into the quiche dish.

Bake at 425 degrees F for 15 minutes.

Reduce the oven temperature to 300 degrees F.

Bake for a further 30 minutes.

Allow the quiche to stand for 10 minutes.

BLUE CHEESE AND PECAN NUT QUICHE

INGREDIENTS

8 eggs
125 ml sour cream
125 ml milk
250 ml blue cheese (crumbled)
125 ml pecan nuts (chopped)
5 ml salt
5 ml ground black pepper

METHOD

Beat the eggs well.

Combine the sour cream and milk together.

Combine the eggs, salt, black pepper and the sour cream mixture together.

Add the blue cheese and pecan nuts.

Mix well.

Pour the mixture into a greased oven dish.

Bake at 350° F for 25 to 30 minutes.

PEPPER QUICHE

INGREDIENTS

2 sweet red peppers (tops cut off and seeds removed)
125 ml frozen vegetables (thawed)
2 eggs
62,5 ml milk
2 ml garlic powder
2 ml Italian seasoning

METHOD

Stand peppers upright in muffin-pan cups.

Spoon the vegetables into each pepper.

Combine the eggs, milk and seasonings together.

Mix until well blended.

Pour the egg mixture over the vegetables in each pepper.

Bake at 325 degree F for 60 to 70 minutes.

Stand for 5 minutes before serving.

SAUSAGE AND CHEESE QUICHE

INGREDIENTS

125 ml butter
80 ml cream cheese
250 ml flour
250 ml cheddar cheese (grated)
1/2 lb sausage (crumbled)
12,5 ml chives (chopped)
2 eggs
250 ml milk
3 ml salt
2 ml cayenne pepper

METHOD

Combine the butter and cream cheese together until creamy.

Add the flour.

Refrigerate for 1 hour.

Press the dough into a greased oven dish.

Brown the sausage in a pan over a medium heat.

Stir occasionally until browned.

Remove from heat and drain off the excess fat.

Sprinkle the sausage evenly into the pastry shell.

Top with the cheddar cheese and chives.

Whisk the eggs, milk, salt and the cayenne pepper together.

Pour the egg mixture over the sausage in the pastry shell.

Bake at 375 degrees F for 20 to 30 minutes.

PIZZA QUICHE

INGREDIENTS

8 eggs
125 ml sour cream
125 ml milk
125 ml Parmesan cheese (grated)
250 ml mozzarella cheese (grated)
5 ml garlic (minced)
5 ml salt
5 ml ground black pepper
250 ml pizza sauce

METHOD

Beat the eggs together.

Combine the sour cream and milk together.

Combine eggs, garlic, salt, black pepper, pizza sauce and sour ream mixture together.

Add the Parmesan cheese and mozzarella cheese.

Mix well.

Pour the mixture into a greased oven dish.

Bake at 350° F for 25 to 30 minutes.

BROCCOLI AND HAM QUICHE

INGREDIENTS

8 eggs
125 ml sour cream
125 ml milk
250 ml cheddar cheese (grated)
250 ml mozzarella cheese (grated)
5 ml salt
5 ml ground black pepper
5 ml mustard powder
5 ml dill
125 ml ham (chopped)
187 ml broccoli

METHOD

Beat the eggs together.

Combine the sour cream and milk together.

Combine eggs, salt, black pepper, mustard powder, dill and sour cream mixture together.

Add the cheddar cheese, ham, broccoli and mozzarella cheese.

Mix well.

Pour the mixture into a greased oven dish.

Bake at 350° F for 25 to 30 minutes.

FETA AND SPINACH QUICHE

INGREDIENTS

8 eggs
125 ml sour cream
125 ml milk
250 ml cheddar cheese (grated)
250 ml feta (crumbled)
5 ml salt
5 ml ground black pepper
187 ml spinach (cooked and drained very well)

METHOD

Beat the eggs together.

Combine the sour cream and milk together.

Combine eggs, salt, black pepper and sour cream mixture together.

Add the cheddar cheese, spinach and feta.

Mix well.

Pour the mixture into a greased oven dish.

Bake at 350° F for 25 to 30 minutes.

BACON AND LEEK QUICHE

INGREDIENTS

300 ml flour
150 ml corn flour
2 ml salt
110 ml butter
1 egg yolk
80 ml cold water
750 g leeks (peeled and sliced)
75 ml oil
125 g bacon (diced)
125 ml sour cream
25 ml corn flour
2 eggs
1 egg white
2 ml caraway seeds
5 ml salt
5 ml ground black pepper
250 ml cheddar cheese (grated)

METHOD

Sift the flour, corn flour and salt together.

Rub in the butter.

Whisk the egg yolk and water together.

Add the water and blend lightly.

Cover the pastry and allow the pastry to stand for 30 minutes in the refrigerator.

Roll the pastry out on a floured board.

Cut the pastry to fit a quiche dish.

Place the pastry in the greased quiche dish.

Pour dried beans into the quiche crust and bake blind at 200 degrees C for 10 minutes.

Remove from the oven and allow the quiche crust to cool.

Remove the beans.

Sauté the leeks and oil together.

Add the bacon and sauté for a further minute.

Remove from heat and allow the mixture to cool.

Spoon the bacon mixture into the baked quiche crust.

Beat the cream, corn flour, eggs, egg white, caraway seeds, salt and black pepper together.

Add the cheese.

Pour the mixture over the leeks.

Bake at 200 degrees C for 20 to 25 minutes.

ROSEMARY, CHICKEN AND MUSHROOM QUICHE

INGREDIENTS

95,5 ml shortening
250 ml flour
2 ml salt
37,5 ml cold water
250 ml chicken (cooked, de-boned and diced)
250 ml canned mushrooms (drained)
250 ml cheddar cheese (grated)
83 ml red onion (peeled and finely chopped)
4 eggs (beaten)
500 ml whipping cream
3 ml salt
2 ml ground black pepper
10 ml fresh rosemary (chopped)
25 ml fresh parsley (chopped)

METHOD

Cut the shortening into the flour and salt.

Add the water 12,5 ml at a time.

Keep adding the water until the pastry almost cleans the side of the bowl (add more water if necessary).

Gather the pastry into a ball and place on a floured board.

Roll the pastry into circles larger than the quiche dish.

Place the pastry into the greased quiche dish.

Trim the overhanging edges of the pastry.

Pinch off the edges to neaten the pastry.

Sprinkle the chicken, mushrooms, cheese and red onion into the pastry-lined quiche dish.

Beat the eggs, cream, salt, rosemary, parsley and black pepper together.

Pour the egg mixture into the quiche dish.

Bake at 425 degrees F for 15 minutes.

Reduce the oven temperature to 300 degrees F.

Bake for a further 30 minutes.

Allow the quiche to stand for 10 minutes.

ASPARAGUS QUICHE

INGREDIENTS

300 ml flour
150 ml corn flour
2 ml salt
110 ml butter
1 egg yolk
80 ml cold water
100 ml butter (melted)
100 ml flour
2 ml salt
250 ml milk
2 eggs (separated)
1 egg white
460 g canned asparagus pieces (drained)
250 ml cheddar cheese (grated)
5 ml mustard powder

METHOD

Sift the flour, corn flour and salt together.

Rub in the butter.

Whisk the egg yolk and water together.

Add the water and blend lightly.

Cover the pastry and allow the pastry to stand for 30 minutes in the refrigerator.

Roll the pastry out on a floured board.

Cut the pastry to fit a quiche dish.

Place the pastry in the greased quiche dish.

Pour dried beans into the quiche crust and bake blind at 200 degrees C for 10 minutes.

Remove from the oven and allow the quiche crust to cool.

Remove the beans.

Combine the melted butter, flour and salt together.

Add the milk and beat until smooth.

Pour into a saucepan and cook while stirring constantly until the mixture has thickened.

Remove from heat.

Beat the egg yolks, egg white and asparagus together.

Combine the white sauce and the asparagus mixture together.

Add the cheese and the mustard powder.

Mix well.

Whisk the egg whites until stiff.

Fold the egg whites into the asparagus mixture.

Pour the filling into the quiche crust.

Bake at 190 degrees C for 20 to 25 minutes.

TUNA AND CORN QUICHE

INGREDIENTS

125 ml butter
80 ml cream cheese
250 ml flour
250 ml cheddar cheese (grated)
1 can tuna (drained)
1 can sweet corn
12,5 ml chives (chopped)
2 eggs
250 ml milk
3 ml salt
2 ml ground black pepper

METHOD

Combine the butter and cream cheese together until creamy.

Add the flour.

Refrigerate for 1 hour.

Press the dough into a greased oven dish.

Combine the tuna, sweet corn, cheddar cheese and chives together.

Pour the mixture into the pastry shell.

Whisk the eggs, milk, salt and the black pepper together.

Pour the egg mixture over the tuna mixture in the pastry shell.

Bake at 375 degrees F for 20 to 30 minutes.

3 CHEESE AND ONION QUICHE

INGREDIENTS

8 eggs
125 ml sour cream
125 ml milk
125 ml feta (crumbled)
250 ml mozzarella cheese (grated)
250 ml cheddar cheese (grated)
2 red onions (peeled and diced)
12,5 ml butter
5 ml salt
5 ml ground black pepper

METHOD

Sauté the butter and onions together until the onions are soft.

Remove from the heat.

Beat the eggs well.

Combine the sour cream and milk together.

Combine the eggs, salt, black pepper and the sour cream mixture together.

Add the cheddar cheese, mozzarella cheese, onion and feta.

Pour the mixture into a greased oven dish.

Bake at 350° F for 25 to 30 minutes.

SPICY CHORIZO SAUSAGE QUICHE

INGREDIENTS

95,5 ml shortening
250 ml flour
2 ml salt
37,5 ml cold water
250 ml chorizo sausage (cooked and thinly sliced)
250 ml strong cheddar cheese (grated)
83 ml red onion (peeled and sliced into rings)
1 red bell pepper (seeded and chopped)
1 red chili (seeded and chopped)
12,5 ml olive oil
4 eggs (beaten)
500 ml whipping cream
3 ml salt
2 ml ground black pepper
25 ml fresh parsley (chopped)
25 ml fresh cilantro (chopped)

METHOD

Cut the shortening into the flour and salt.

Add the water 12,5 ml at a time.

Keep adding the water until the pastry almost cleans the side of the bowl (add more water if necessary).

Gather the pastry into a ball and place on a floured board.

Roll the pastry into circles larger than the quiche dish.

Place the pastry into the greased quiche dish.

Trim the overhanging edges of the pastry.

Pinch off the edges to neaten the pastry.

Sauté the olive oil, red pepper, red chili and red onion together until the onion is soft.

Remove from the heat.

Sprinkle the chorizo sausage, cheese, parsley, cilantro and red onion mixture into the pastry-lined quiche dish.

Beat the eggs, cream, salt and black pepper together.

Pour the egg mixture into the quiche dish.

Bake at 425 degrees F for 15 minutes.

Reduce the oven temperature to 300 degrees F.

Bake for a further 30 minutes.

Allow the quiche to stand for 10 minutes.

CRANBERRY, WALNUT AND BRIE QUICHE

INGREDIENTS

8 eggs
125 ml sour cream
125 ml milk
250 ml Brie (cut in pieces)
250 ml walnuts (chopped)
250 ml cranberries
5 ml salt
5 ml ground black pepper

METHOD

Beat the eggs well.

Combine the sour cream and milk together.

Combine the eggs, salt, black pepper and the sour cream mixture together.

Add the walnut pieces, pieces of Brie and cranberries.

Mix well.

Pour the mixture into a greased oven dish.

Bake at 350° F for 25 to 30 minutes.

CHICKEN AND LEEK QUICHE

INGREDIENTS

8 eggs
125 ml sour cream
125 ml milk
250 ml cheddar cheese (grated)
250 ml chicken (cooked and diced)
250 ml leeks (cleaned and sliced)
12,5 ml butter
5 ml salt
5 ml ground black pepper

METHOD

Sauté the butter and leeks until the leeks are soft.

Remove from the heat.

Beat the eggs well.

Combine the sour cream and milk together.

Combine the eggs, salt, black pepper and the sour cream mixture together.

Add the cheddar cheese, chicken and leeks.

Mix well.

Pour the mixture into a greased oven dish.

Bake at 350° F for 25 to 30 minutes.

BACON AND ZUCCHINI QUICHE

INGREDIENTS

    125 ml butter
    80 ml cream cheese
    250 ml flour
    250 ml cheddar cheese (grated)
    250 ml bacon (diced)
    250 ml zucchini (tops and bottoms cut off, sliced)
    12,5 ml butter
    1 onion (peeled and chopped)
    2 eggs
    250 ml milk
    3 ml salt
    2 ml ground black pepper

METHOD

Combine the butter and cream cheese together until creamy.

Add the flour.

Refrigerate for 1 hour.

Press the dough into a greased oven dish.

Sauté the butter, bacon and onion until the onion is soft.

Add the zucchini.

Sauté for a minute or 2 more.

Remove from the heat.

Sprinkle the bacon mixture evenly into the pastry shell.

Top with the cheddar cheese.

Whisk the eggs, milk, salt and the black pepper together.

Pour the egg mixture over the bacon in the pastry shell.

Bake at 375 degrees F for 20 to 30 minutes.

GRUYERE, BACON AND MAPLE QUICHE

INGREDIENTS

125 ml butter
80 ml cream cheese
250 ml flour
250 ml Gruyere cheese (grated)
250 ml bacon (diced)
25 ml maple syrup
2 eggs
250 ml milk
3 ml salt

METHOD

Combine the butter and cream cheese together until creamy.

Add the flour.

Refrigerate for 1 hour.

Press the dough into a greased oven dish.

Sauté the bacon until the bacon has browned.

Remove from the heat.

Pour off excess fat.

Sprinkle the bacon evenly into the pastry shell.

Top with the Gruyere cheese.

Whisk the eggs, milk, salt, maple syrup and the cayenne pepper together.

Pour the egg mixture over the bacon in the pastry shell.

Bake at 375 degrees F for 20 to 30 minutes.

LAMB AND MINT QUICHE

INGREDIENTS

95,5 ml shortening
250 ml flour
2 ml salt
37,5 ml cold water
250 ml lamb (cooked and diced)
125 ml sun dried tomatoes (chopped)
250 ml Gruyere (grated)
83 ml onion (peeled and finely chopped)
4 eggs (beaten)
500 ml whipping cream
3 ml salt
2 ml ground black pepper
25 ml fresh parsley (chopped)
25 ml fresh mint (chopped)

METHOD

Cut the shortening into the flour and salt.

Add the water 12,5 ml at a time.

Keep adding the water until the pastry almost cleans the side of the bowl (add more water if necessary).

Gather the pastry into a ball and place on a floured board.

Roll the pastry into circles larger than the quiche dish.

Place the pastry into the greased quiche dish.

Trim the overhanging edges of the pastry.

Pinch off the edges to neaten the pastry.

Sprinkle the lamb, sun dried tomatoes, cheese, mint, parsley and onion into the pastry-lined quiche dish.

Beat the eggs, cream, salt and black pepper together.

Pour the egg mixture into the quiche dish.

Bake at 425 degrees F for 15 minutes.

Reduce the oven temperature to 300 degrees F.

Bake for a further 30 minutes.

Allow the quiche to stand for 10 minutes.

BLUE CHEESE AND FRESH HERB QUICHE

INGREDIENTS

    8 eggs
    125 ml sour cream
    125 ml milk
    250 ml blue cheese (crumbled)
    5 ml salt
    5 ml ground black pepper
    12, 5 ml fresh parsley (chopped)
    12,5 ml fresh thyme (chopped)
    12,5 ml fresh tarragon (chopped)
    12,5 ml fresh chives (chopped)

METHOD

Beat the eggs well.

Combine the sour cream and milk together.

Combine the eggs, salt, black pepper, parsley, thyme, tarragon, chives and the sour cream mixture together.

Add the blue cheese.

Mix well.

Pour the mixture into a greased oven dish.

Bake at 350° F for 25 to 30 minutes.

MUSHROOM GRUYERE QUICHE

INGREDIENTS

125 ml butter
80 ml cream cheese
250 ml flour
750 g fresh mushrooms (cleaned and chopped)
2 onions (peeled and chopped)
50 ml fresh parsley (chopped)
50 ml oil
250 ml Gruyere cheese (grated)
3 eggs
125 ml sour cream
5 ml salt
4 ml ground black pepper

METHOD

Combine the butter and cream cheese together until creamy.

Add the flour.

Refrigerate for 1 hour.

Press the dough into a greased oven dish.

Sauté the mushrooms, onions, parsley and oil together until the onions are soft.

Remove from the heat.

Allow the mushroom mixture to cool.

Beat the eggs, sour cream, salt and black pepper together.

Combine the mushroom mixture and the egg mixture together.

Add the Gruyere cheese.

Mix well.

Pout the mixture into the crust.

Bake at 375 degrees F for 20 to 30 minutes.

SEAFOOD QUICHE

INGREDIENTS

95,5 ml shortening
250 ml flour
2 ml salt
37,5 ml cold water
83 ml crabmeat (picked and chopped)
83 ml shrimp
83 ml salmon (chopped)
250 ml Gruyere (grated)
83 ml green onion (peeled and finely chopped)
4 eggs (beaten)
500 ml whipping cream
5 ml salt
2 ml ground black pepper
2 ml cayenne pepper

METHOD

Cut the shortening into the flour and salt.

Add the water 12,5 ml at a time.

Keep adding the water until the pastry almost cleans the side of the bowl (add more water if necessary).

Gather the pastry into a ball and place on a floured board.

Roll the pastry into circles larger than the quiche dish.

Place the pastry into the greased quiche dish.

Trim the overhanging edges of the pastry.

Pinch off the edges to neaten the pastry.

Sprinkle the crabmeat, shrimp, salmon, cheese and green onion into the pastry-lined quiche dish.

Beat the eggs, cream, salt, black pepper and cayenne pepper together.

Pour the egg mixture into the quiche dish.

Bake at 425 degrees F for 15 minutes.

Reduce the oven temperature to 300 degrees F.

Bake for a further 30 minutes.

Allow the quiche to stand for 10 minutes.

SWEET CHILI CRAB QUICHE

INGREDIENTS

125 ml butter
80 ml cream cheese
250 ml flour
250 ml cheddar cheese (grated)
12,5 ml chives (chopped)
187 ml sweet chili sauce
500 ml crabmeat (thawed if frozen, picked and diced)
3 eggs
250 ml milk
3 ml salt
2 ml ground black pepper

METHOD

Combine the butter and cream cheese together until creamy.

Add the flour.

Refrigerate for 1 hour.

Press the dough into a greased oven dish.

Combine the cheddar cheese, crabmeat, sweet chili sauce and chives together.

Pour the mixture into the pastry shell.

Whisk the eggs, milk, salt and the black pepper together.

Pour the egg mixture over the crab mixture in the pastry shell.

Bake at 375 degrees F for 20 to 30 minutes.

CARAMELIZED ONION, FETA AND WALNUT QUICHE

INGREDIENTS

125 ml butter
80 ml cream cheese
250 ml flour
250 ml walnuts (chopped)
250 ml feta (crumbled)
250 ml onions (peeled and sliced into rings)
12,5 ml butter
3 eggs
250 ml milk
3 ml salt
2 ml ground black pepper

METHOD

Combine the butter and cream cheese together until creamy.

Add the flour.

Refrigerate for 1 hour.

Press the dough into a greased oven dish.

Sauté the onions and butter together until the onions are browned (at least 30 minutes).

Stir occasionally to prevent burning.

Combine the feta, caramelised onions and walnuts together.

Pour the mixture into the pastry shell.

Whisk the eggs, milk, salt and the black pepper together.

Pour the egg mixture over the feta mixture in the pastry shell.

Bake at 375 degrees F for 20 to 30 minutes.

MINI BACON AND CHEESE QUICHES

INGREDIENTS

200 g pastry
500 g bacon (diced)
250 ml cheddar cheese (grated)
5 ml mustard powder
2 ml red pepper
4 eggs (beaten)
60 ml milk

METHOD

Roll out the pastry on a floured board and cut out circles with a cookie cutter.

Press the circles into a greased miniature muffin pan.

Combine the remaining ingredients together.

Spoon the mixture into the pastry circles.

Bake at 180 degrees C for 25 to 30 minutes.

LOBSTER QUICHE

INGREDIENTS

125 ml butter
80 ml cream cheese
250 ml flour
500 ml lobster (minced)
50 ml béchamel sauce
5 ml anchovy sauce
10 ml lemon juice
3 ml cayenne pepper
3 ml salt
2 ml ground black pepper
3 eggs
250 ml milk

METHOD

Combine the butter and cream cheese together until creamy.

Add the flour.

Refrigerate for 1 hour.

Press the dough into a greased oven dish.

Combine the lobster, béchamel sauce, anchovy sauce, lemon juice, cayenne pepper, black pepper and salt together

Pour the mixture into the pastry shell.

Whisk the eggs and milk together.

Pour the egg mixture over the lobster mixture in the pastry shell.

Bake at 375 degrees F for 20 to 30 minutes.

APPLE, WALNUT AND BLUE CHEESE QUICHE

INGREDIENTS

8 eggs
125 ml sour cream
125 ml milk
250 ml blue cheese (crumbled)
250 ml canned apple (drained and chopped)
125 ml walnuts (chopped)
12,5 ml chives (chopped)
5 ml salt
5 ml ground black pepper

METHOD

Beat the eggs well.

Combine the sour cream and milk together.

Combine the eggs, salt, black pepper and the sour cream mixture together.

Add the blue cheese, apple, chives and walnuts.

Mix well.

Pour the mixture into a greased oven dish.

Bake at 350° F for 25 to 30 minutes.

GRUYERE, PEAR AND HAM QUICHE

INGREDIENTS

125 ml butter
80 ml cream cheese
250 ml flour
250 ml Gruyere cheese (grated)
250 ml canned pears (drained and chopped)
250 ml ham (diced)
12,5 ml chives (chopped)
3 eggs
250 ml milk
5 ml salt
5 ml ground black pepper

METHOD

Combine the butter and cream cheese together until creamy.

Add the flour.

Refrigerate for 1 hour.

Press the dough into a greased oven dish.

Place the pears and ham evenly into the pastry shell.

Top with the Gruyere cheese and chives.

Whisk the eggs, milk, salt and the black pepper together.

Pour the egg mixture over the ham and pears in the pastry shell.

Bake at 375 degrees F for 20 to 30 minutes.

ARTICHOKE QUICHE

INGREDIENTS

300 ml flour
150 ml corn flour
2 ml salt
110 ml butter
1 egg yolk
80 ml cold water
250 ml Mozzarella cheese (grated)
125 ml Parmesan cheese (grated)
250 ml milk
3 eggs (beaten)
250 ml artichoke hearts (drained and chopped)
1 onion (peeled and chopped)
5 ml salt
5 ml ground black pepper

METHOD

Sift the flour, corn flour and salt together.

Rub in the butter.

Whisk the egg yolk and water together.

Add the water and blend lightly.

Cover the pastry and allow the pastry to stand for 30 minutes in the refrigerator.

Roll the pastry out on a floured board.

Cut the pastry to fit a quiche dish.

Place the pastry in the greased quiche dish.

Pour dried beans into the quiche crust and bake blind at 200 degrees C for 10 minutes.

Remove from the oven and allow the quiche crust to cool.

Remove the beans.

Combine the mozzarella cheese, Parmesan cheese, milk, eggs, artichokes, onion, salt and black pepper together.

Pour the mixture into the quiche crust.

Bake at 180 degrees C for 20 to 25 minutes.

ZUCCHINI AND RED PEPPER QUICHE

INGREDIENTS

8 eggs
125 ml sour cream
125 ml milk
250 ml cheddar cheese (grated)
5 ml salt
5 ml ground black pepper
25 ml fresh cilantro (chopped)
500 ml zucchini (tops and bottoms cut off and sliced)
1 red bell pepper (seeded and chopped)
1 red onion (peeled and chopped)
2 red chilies (seeded and minced)
12,5 ml limejuice
12,5 ml olive oil

METHOD

Sauté the red onions, red bell pepper and olive oil together until the onions are soft.

Remove from the heat.

Allow the onion mixture to cool.

Beat the eggs well.

Combine the sour cream and milk together.

Combine the eggs, salt, black pepper and the sour cream mixture together.

Add the zucchini, cilantro, onion mixture, red chillies, cheddar cheese and limejuice.

Mix well.

Pour the mixture into a greased oven dish.

Bake at 350° F for 25 to 30 minutes.

BLUEBERRY, FETA AND ALMOND QUICHE

INGREDIENTS

8 eggs
125 ml sour cream
125 ml milk
250 ml feta (crumbled)
125 ml almonds (chopped)
250 ml blueberries
5 ml salt
5 ml ground black pepper
37,5 ml fresh parsley (chopped)

METHOD

Beat the eggs well.

Combine the sour cream and milk together.

Combine the eggs, salt, black pepper and the sour cream mixture together.

Add the feta, blueberries, parsley and almonds.

Mix well.

Pour the mixture into a greased oven dish.

Bake at 350° F for 25 to 30 minutes.

BACON AND OYSTER QUICHE

INGREDIENTS

125 ml butter
80 ml cream cheese
250 ml flour
1 green pepper (seeded and chopped)
12,5 ml olive oil
250 ml bacon (diced)
250 ml canned oysters (drained)
37,5 ml fresh parsley (chopped)
25 ml chives (chopped)
250 ml cheddar cheese (grated)
5 ml salt
5 ml ground black pepper
3 eggs
250 ml milk

METHOD

Combine the butter and cream cheese together until creamy.

Add the flour.

Refrigerate for 1 hour.

Press the dough into a greased oven dish.

Sauté the bacon, green pepper and olive oil until the bacon has browned.

Remove from the heat.

Allow the bacon to cool.

Sprinkle the bacon mixture and oysters evenly into the pastry shell.

Top with the cheddar cheese, parsley and chives.

Whisk the eggs, milk, salt and the black pepper together.

Pour the egg mixture over the bacon and oyster mixture

Bake at 375 degrees F for 20 to 30 minutes.

EGGPLANT, HAM AND MOZZARELLA QUICHE

INGREDIENTS

250 ml eggplant (peeled and diced)
5 ml salt
Olive oil to fry eggplant
1 onion (peeled and chopped)
5 ml garlic (minced)
8 eggs
125 ml sour cream
125 ml milk
5 ml salt
5 ml ground black pepper
250 ml mozzarella cheese (chopped)
250 ml ham (diced)

METHOD

Combine the eggplant and salt together.

Allow the eggplant to stand for 30 minutes.

Drain the eggplant and pat dry with paper towels.

Heat the olive oil in a pan.

When the olive oil is very hot but not smoking add the eggplant.

Cook the eggplant for 4 to 8 minutes.

Turn frequently. The eggplant must be tender but not mushy.

Add the onions and garlic.

Cook for 1 minute.

Remove from the heat.

Drain the eggplant and onion from the olive oil.

Beat the eggs well.

Combine the sour cream and milk together.

Combine the eggs, salt, black pepper and the sour cream mixture together.

Add the mozzarella cheese, eggplant mixture and ham.

Mix well.

Pour the mixture into a greased oven dish.

Bake at 350° F for 25 to 30 minutes.

POTATO QUICHE

INGREDIENTS

125 ml butter
80 ml cream cheese
250 ml flour
50 ml butter
1 red onion (peeled and chopped)
2 cloves garlic (peeled and chopped)
2 potatoes (peeled, boiled and grated)
3 eggs
5 ml salt
5 ml ground black pepper
50 g ham (diced)
50 ml cheddar cheese (grated)
3 spring onions (cleaned and chopped)
37,5 ml fresh parsley (chopped)

METHOD

Combine the butter and cream cheese together until creamy.

Add the flour.

Refrigerate for 1 hour.

Press the dough into a greased oven dish.

Sauté the butter and onion together until the onion is tender.

Add the garlic and potatoes.

Cook for 5 minutes.

Remove from the heat.

Beat the eggs, ham, cheddar cheese, salt, black pepper, parsley and spring onion together.

Combine the egg mixture and the onion mixture together.

Pour the mixture into the quiche crust.

Bake at 180 degrees C for 1 hour.

SALMON, DILL AND FETA QUICHE

INGREDIENTS

300 ml flour
150 ml corn flour
2 ml salt
110 ml butter
1 egg yolk
80 ml cold water
500 ml smoked salmon (chopped)
5 ml lemon juice
25 ml fresh dill (chopped)
25 ml fresh parsley (chopped)
250 ml feta (crumbled)
3 eggs
5 ml salt
5 ml ground black pepper
250 ml milk

METHOD

Sift the flour, corn flour and salt together.

Rub in the butter.

Whisk the egg yolk and water together.

Add the water and blend lightly.

Cover the pastry and allow the pastry to stand for 30 minutes in the refrigerator.

Roll the pastry out on a floured board.

Cut the pastry to fit a quiche dish.

Place the pastry in the greased quiche dish.

Pour dried beans into the quiche crust and bake blind at 200 degrees C for 10 minutes.

Remove from the oven and allow the quiche crust to cool.

Remove the beans.

Place the smoked salmon in the quiche crust.

Drizzle lemon juice over the salmon.

Sprinkle the feta, parsley and dill over the salmon.

Beat the eggs, salt, black pepper and milk together.

Pour the egg mixture over the salmon.

Bake at 180 degrees C for 20 to 25 minutes.

TOMATO AND FRESH BASIL QUICHE

INGREDIENTS

300 ml flour
150 ml corn flour
2 ml salt
110 ml butter
1 egg yolk
80 ml cold water
400 g cherry tomatoes (cut in half)
125 ml Parmesan cheese (grated)
250 ml Mozzarella cheese (grated)
7,5 ml basil pesto
3 ml garlic (crushed)
25 ml pine nuts
25 ml fresh basil leaves (chopped)
3 eggs
250 ml sour cream
5 ml salt
5 ml ground black pepper

METHOD

Sift the flour, corn flour and salt together.

Rub in the butter.

Whisk the egg yolk and water together.

Add the water and blend lightly.

Cover the pastry and allow the pastry to stand for 30 minutes in the refrigerator.

Roll the pastry out on a floured board.

Cut the pastry to fit a quiche dish.

Place the pastry in the greased quiche dish.

Pour dried beans into the quiche crust and bake blind at 200 degrees C for 10 minutes.

Remove from the oven and allow the quiche crust to cool.

Remove the beans.

Place the cherry tomatoes in the baked quiche crust.

Sprinkle the Parmesan cheese, mozzarella cheese, pine nuts, basil leaves and garlic on top of the tomatoes.

Beat the eggs, sour cream, basil pesto, salt and black pepper together.

Pour the egg mixture over the cheese.

Bake at 180 degrees C for 20 to 25 minutes.

BUTTERNUT, FETA AND BACON QUICHE

INGREDIENTS

8 eggs
125 ml sour cream
125 ml milk
250 ml feta (crumbled)
250 ml bacon (fried and diced)
37,5 ml fresh parsley (chopped)
1 butternut (peeled, seeded and thinly sliced)
25 ml chives (chopped)
5 ml salt
5 ml ground black pepper

METHOD

Beat the eggs well.

Combine the sour cream and milk together.

Combine the eggs, salt, black pepper and the sour cream mixture together.

Add the feta, parsley, chives, butternut slices and bacon.

Mix well.

Pour the mixture into a greased oven dish.

Bake at 350° F for 35 to 45 minutes.

CHICKEN, WALNUT AND PEAR QUICHE

INGREDIENTS

125 ml butter
80 ml cream cheese
250 ml flour
125 ml walnuts (chopped)
500 ml chicken (cooked and diced)
250 ml canned pears (drained)
250 ml Gruyere cheese (grated)
25 ml chives (chopped)
3 eggs
250 ml milk
5 ml salt
5 ml ground black pepper

METHOD

Combine the butter and cream cheese together until creamy.

Add the flour.

Refrigerate for 1 hour.

Press the dough into a greased oven dish.

Sprinkle the chicken and pears evenly into the pastry shell.

Top with the Gruyere cheese, walnuts and chives.

Whisk the eggs, milk, salt and the black pepper together.

Pour the egg mixture over the sausage in the pastry shell.

Bake at 375 degrees F for 20 to 30 minutes.

SALMON AND PEA QUICHE

INGREDIENTS

125 ml butter
80 ml cream cheese
250 ml flour
500 ml smoked salmon (chopped)
5 ml lemon juice
250 ml frozen peas
25 ml fresh dill (chopped)
250 ml feta (crumbled)
3 eggs
250 ml milk
5 ml salt
5 ml ground black pepper

METHOD

Combine the butter and cream cheese together until creamy.

Add the flour.

Refrigerate for 1 hour.

Press the dough into a greased oven dish.

Sprinkle the salmon evenly into the pastry shell.

Drizzle lemon juice over the salmon.

Top with the frozen peas, feta and dill.

Whisk the eggs, milk, salt and the black pepper together.

Pour the egg mixture over the sausage in the pastry shell.

Bake at 375 degrees F for 20 to 30 minutes.

QUICHE LORRAINE

INGREDIENTS

95,5 ml shortening
250 ml flour
2 ml salt
37,5 ml cold water
8 slices bacon (cooked and crumbled)
250 ml Gruyere (grated)
83 ml onion (peeled and finely chopped)
4 eggs (beaten)
500 ml whipping cream
3 ml salt
2 ml ground black pepper
2 ml cayenne pepper

METHOD

Cut the shortening into the flour and salt.

Add the water 12,5 ml at a time.

Keep adding the water until the pastry almost cleans the side of the bowl (add more water if necessary).

Gather the pastry into a ball and place on a floured board.

Roll the pastry into circles larger than the quiche dish.

Place the pastry into the greased quiche dish.

Trim the overhanging edges of the pastry.

Pinch off the edges to neaten the pastry.

Sprinkle the bacon, cheese and onion into the pastry-lined quiche dish.

Beat the eggs, cream, salt, black pepper and cayenne pepper together.

Pour the egg mixture into the quiche dish.

Bake at 425 degrees F for 15 minutes.

Reduce the oven temperature to 300 degrees F.

Bake for a further 30 minutes.

Allow the quiche to stand for 10 minutes.

HADDOCK AND CORN QUICHE

INGREDIENTS

95,5 ml shortening
250 ml flour
2 ml salt
37,5 ml cold water
250 ml haddock (cooked, de-boned and flaked)
250 ml Gruyere (grated)
250 ml whole kernel corn
83 ml red onion (peeled and finely chopped)
4 eggs (beaten)
500 ml whipping cream
3 ml salt
2 ml ground black pepper
5 ml mustard powder

METHOD

Cut the shortening into the flour and salt.

Add the water 12,5 ml at a time.

Keep adding the water until the pastry almost cleans the side of the bowl (add more water if necessary).

Gather the pastry into a ball and place on a floured board.

Roll the pastry into circles larger than the quiche dish.

Place the pastry into the greased quiche dish.

Trim the overhanging edges of the pastry.

Pinch off the edges to neaten the pastry.

Sprinkle the haddock, whole kernel corn, cheese and red onion into the pastry-lined quiche dish.

Beat the eggs, cream, salt, black pepper and mustard powder together.

Pour the egg mixture into the quiche dish.

Bake at 425 degrees F for 15 minutes.

Reduce the oven temperature to 300 degrees F.

Bake for a further 30 minutes.

Allow the quiche to stand for 10 minutes.

GORGONZOLA AND CARAMELIZED ONION QUICHE

INGREDIENTS

95,5 ml shortening
250 ml flour
2 ml salt
37,5 ml cold water
250 ml red onion (peeled and sliced into rings)
1 red bell pepper (seeded and chopped)
25 ml olive oil
250 ml Gorgonzola cheese (crumbled)
4 eggs (beaten)
500 ml whipping cream
3 ml salt
2 ml ground black pepper
25 ml fresh parsley (chopped)
25 ml fresh thyme (chopped)

METHOD

Cut the shortening into the flour and salt.

Add the water 12,5 ml at a time.

Keep adding the water until the pastry almost cleans the side of the bowl (add more water if necessary).

Gather the pastry into a ball and place on a floured board.

Roll the pastry into circles larger than the quiche dish.

Place the pastry into the greased quiche dish.

Trim the overhanging edges of the pastry.

Pinch off the edges to neaten the pastry.

Sauté the red onion, red bell pepper and olive oil until the onion has caramelised (at least 15 to 20 minutes).

Stir occasionally to prevent burning.

Remove from heat.

Sprinkle the cheese, parsley, thyme and onion mixture into the pastry-lined quiche dish.

Beat the eggs, cream, salt and black pepper together.

Pour the egg mixture into the quiche dish.

Bake at 425 degrees F for 15 minutes.

Reduce the oven temperature to 300 degrees F.

Bake for a further 30 minutes.

Allow the quiche to stand for 10 minutes.

PANCETTA AND ASPARAGUS QUICHE

INGREDIENTS

8 eggs
125 ml sour cream
125 ml milk
250 ml Pancetta (diced)
125 ml Parmesan cheese (grated)
250 ml feta (crumbled)
Fresh asparagus
1 onion (peeled, chopped)
12,5 ml olive oil
5 ml salt
5 ml ground black pepper
25 ml fresh parsley

METHOD

Sauté the olive oil, Pancetta and onion together until the onion is soft and the Pancetta has browned.

Remove from heat.

Beat the eggs well.

Combine the sour cream and milk together.

Combine the eggs, salt, black pepper and the sour cream mixture together.

Add the Parmesan cheese, feta, parsley and Pancetta.

Mix well.

Arrange the fresh asparagus in the greased quiche dish.

Pour the quiche mixture over the asparagus.

Bake at 350° F for 25 to 30 minutes.

TURKEY AND BROCCOLI QUICHE

INGREDIENTS

125 ml butter
80 ml cream cheese
250 ml flour
500 ml turkey (cooked and diced)
250 ml frozen broccoli (thawed)
250 ml Gruyere (grated)
3 eggs
250 ml milk
5 ml salt
5 ml ground black pepper
25 ml fresh parsley (chopped)

METHOD

Combine the butter and cream cheese together until creamy.

Add the flour.

Refrigerate for 1 hour.

Press the dough into a greased oven dish.

Sprinkle the turkey evenly into the pastry shell.

Top with the broccoli, parsley and Gruyere cheese.

Whisk the eggs, milk, salt and the black pepper together.

Pour the egg mixture over the sausage in the pastry shell.

Bake at 375 degrees F for 20 to 30 minutes.

SAGE, APPLE AND SAUSAGE QUICHE

INGREDIENTS

8 eggs
125 ml sour cream
125 ml milk
250 ml cheddar cheese (grated)
1 Granny Smith apple (washed, un-peeled and sliced)
5 ml salt
5 sausage links (cooked and sliced)
5 ml ground black pepper
1 ml sage
5 ml mustard powder

METHOD

Beat the eggs well.

Combine the sour cream and milk together.

Combine the eggs, salt, sage, mustard powder, black pepper and the sour cream mixture together.

Add the cheddar cheese and sausage slices.

Mix well.

Arrange the apple slices in the greased quiche dish.

Pour the quiche mixture over the apple slices.

Bake at 350° F for 25 to 30 minutes.

ARTICHOKE, LEMON THYME AND PARMESAN QUICHE

INGREDIENTS

8 eggs
125 ml sour cream
125 ml milk
125 ml Parmesan cheese (grated)
250 ml Mozzarella cheesed (grated)
250 ml artichoke hearts (drained and chopped)
5 ml salt
5 ml ground black pepper
25 ml fresh lemon thyme (minced)
5 spring onions (cleaned and chopped)

METHOD

Beat the eggs well.

Combine the sour cream and milk together.

Combine the eggs, salt, black pepper and the sour cream mixture together.

Add the Parmesan cheese, mozzarella cheese, lemon thyme, spring onions and the artichokes.

Mix well.

Pour the mixture into the greased quiche dish.

Bake at 350° F for 25 to 30 minutes.

GORGONZOLA AND ROASTED FIG QUICHE

INGREDIENTS

95,5 ml shortening
250 ml flour
2 ml salt
37,5 ml cold water
250 ml Gorgonzola cheese (crumbled)
125 ml walnuts (chopped)
5 fresh figs (cut in half)
4 eggs (beaten)
500 ml whipping cream
3 ml salt
2 ml ground black pepper

METHOD

Cut the shortening into the flour and salt.

Add the water 12,5 ml at a time.

Keep adding the water until the pastry almost cleans the side of the bowl (add more water if necessary).

Gather the pastry into a ball and place on a floured board.

Roll the pastry into circles larger than the quiche dish.

Place the pastry into the greased quiche dish.

Trim the overhanging edges of the pastry.

Pinch off the edges to neaten the pastry.

Arrange the figs in the pastry-lined quiche dish.

Sprinkle the cheese and walnuts over the figs.

Beat the eggs, cream, salt and black pepper together.

Pour the egg mixture into the quiche dish.

Bake at 425 degrees F for 15 minutes.

Reduce the oven temperature to 300 degrees F.

Bake for a further 30 minutes.

FETA, STRAWBERRY AND BLACK PEPPER QUICHE

INGREDIENTS

95,5 ml shortening
250 ml flour
2 ml salt
37,5 ml cold water
250 ml fresh strawberries (cut in half)
250 ml Feta (crumbled)
4 eggs (beaten)
500 ml whipping cream
3 ml salt
5 ml fresh ground black pepper
25 ml fresh parsley (chopped)
25 ml fresh basil (chopped)

METHOD

Cut the shortening into the flour and salt.

Add the water 12,5 ml at a time.

Keep adding the water until the pastry almost cleans the side of the bowl (add more water if necessary).

Gather the pastry into a ball and place on a floured board.

Roll the pastry into circles larger than the quiche dish.

Place the pastry into the greased quiche dish.

Trim the overhanging edges of the pastry.

Pinch off the edges to neaten the pastry.

Arrange the strawberries in the pastry-lined quiche dish.

Sprinkle the feta, parsley, basil and black pepper over the strawberries

Beat the eggs, cream and salt together.

Pour the egg mixture into the quiche dish.

Bake at 425 degrees F for 15 minutes.

Reduce the oven temperature to 300 degrees F.

Bake for a further 30 minutes.

CHICKEN AND CASHEW QUICHE

INGREDIENTS

95,5 ml shortening
250 ml flour
2 ml salt
37,5 ml cold water
250 ml chicken (cooked and diced)
125 ml sun-dried tomatoes (chopped)
125 ml cashews
25 ml fresh tarragon (chopped)
250 ml Gruyere cheese (grated)
4 eggs (beaten)
500 ml whipping cream
3 ml salt
3 ml ground black pepper

METHOD

Cut the shortening into the flour and salt.

Add the water 12,5 ml at a time.

Keep adding the water until the pastry almost cleans the side of the bowl (add more water if necessary).

Gather the pastry into a ball and place on a floured board.

Roll the pastry into circles larger than the quiche dish.

Place the pastry into the greased quiche dish.

Trim the overhanging edges of the pastry.

Pinch off the edges to neaten the pastry.

Arrange the chicken and sun-dried tomatoes in the pastry-lined quiche dish.

Sprinkle the cheese, tarragon and cashews over the chicken.

Beat the eggs, cream, black pepper and salt together.

Pour the egg mixture into the quiche dish.

Bake at 425 degrees F for 15 minutes.

Reduce the oven temperature to 300 degrees F.

Bake for a further 30 minutes.

Printed in Great Britain
by Amazon